Zoom In on

Backyard Animals

# Grasshoppers

Leo Statts

**abdopublishing.com**

Published by Abdo Zoom™, PO Box 398166, Minneapolis, Minnesota 55439. 

Printed in the United States of America, North Mankato, Minnesota
052017
092017

THIS BOOK CONTAINS
RECYCLED MATERIALS

Cover Photo: Image Depot Pro/iStockphoto
Interior Photos: Melinda Fawver/iStockphoto, 1; Shutterstock Images, 4–5, 16, 17; iStockphoto, 5, 6, 7, 8–9, 10, 12, 14–15, 18–19; Red Line Editorial, 9, 20 (left), 20 (right), 21 (left), 21 (right); Major Designs/iStockphoto, 13; Antonio Clemens/iStockphoto, 18

Editor: Brienna Rossiter
Series Designer: Madeline Berger
Art Direction: Dorothy Toth

**Publishers Cataloging-in-Publication Data**
Names: Statts, Leo, author.
Title: Grasshoppers / by Leo Statts.
Description: Minneapolis, MN : Abdo Zoom, 2018. | Series: Backyard animals | Includes bibliographical references and index.
Identifiers: LCCN 2017931134 | ISBN 9781532120053 (lib. bdg.) | ISBN 9781614797166 (ebook) | ISBN 9781614797722 (Read-to-me ebook)
Subjects: LCSH: Grasshoppers--Juvenile literature. | Insects--Juvenile literature.
Classification: DDC 595.7--dc23
LC record available at http://lccn.loc.gov/2017931134

# Table of Contents

# Grasshoppers

Grasshoppers are insects.
They have six legs.

They use their two back legs to jump far and high.

# Body

Grasshoppers have two **antennae**.

Most grasshoppers are green or brown. Some have black, red, or yellow spots.

# Habitat

Grasshoppers live in many places around the world. They are often found in **grasslands**. Others live in mountains or **deserts**.

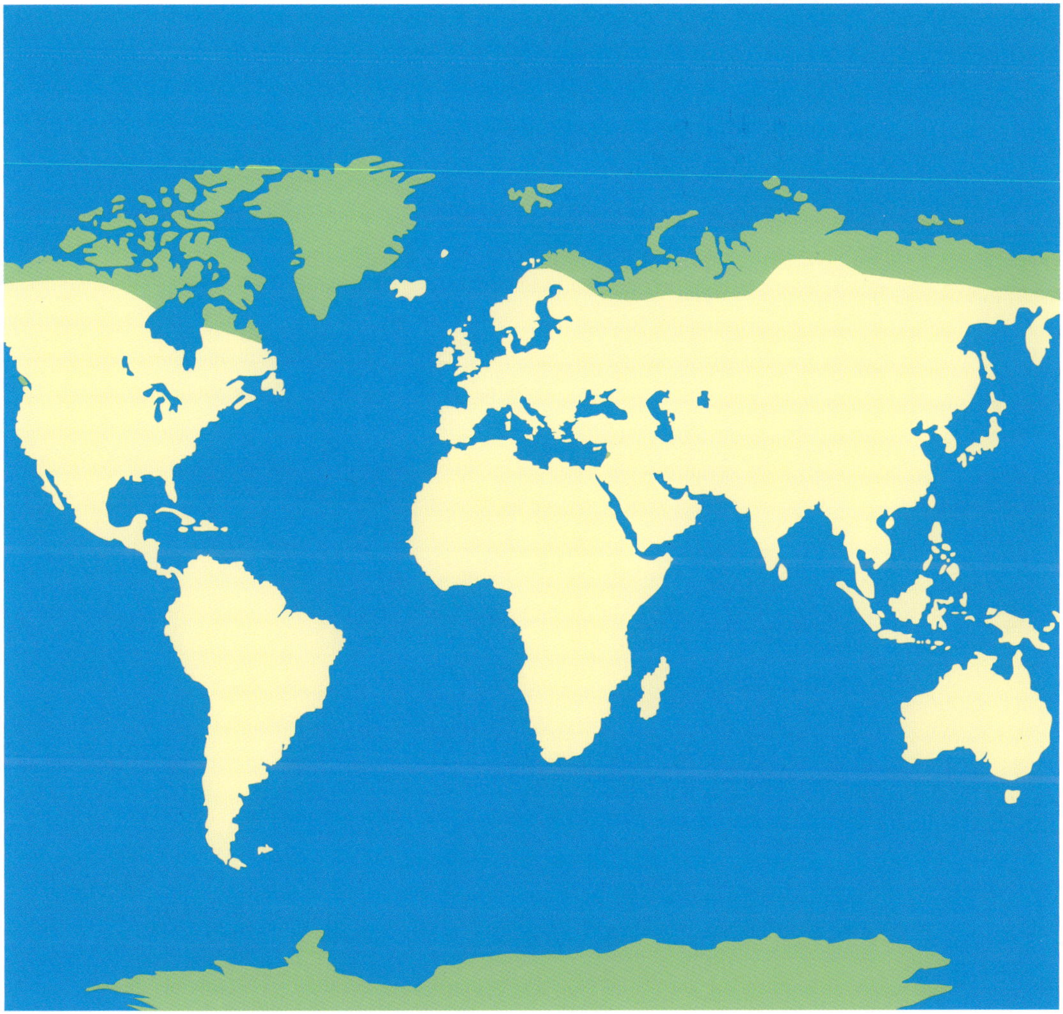

Where grasshoppers live

You might find grasshoppers in your garden, too. Grasshoppers **migrate** when it gets cold.

# Food

Grasshoppers eat plants.

They often eat grass. They also eat seeds, leaves, and bark.

Sometimes grasshoppers move and eat together in large groups. This is called swarming.

# Life Cycle

Female grasshoppers lay eggs in holes in the dirt.

Babies **hatch** from the eggs in the spring. They are called **nymphs**.

Nymphs shed their skin as they grow. Soon they become adults.

Grasshoppers live for about four months.

Quick Stats

## Smallest Size

A pygmy grasshopper is shorter than a penny.

Quick Stats

## Largest Size

The largest grasshopper is longer than a baseball.

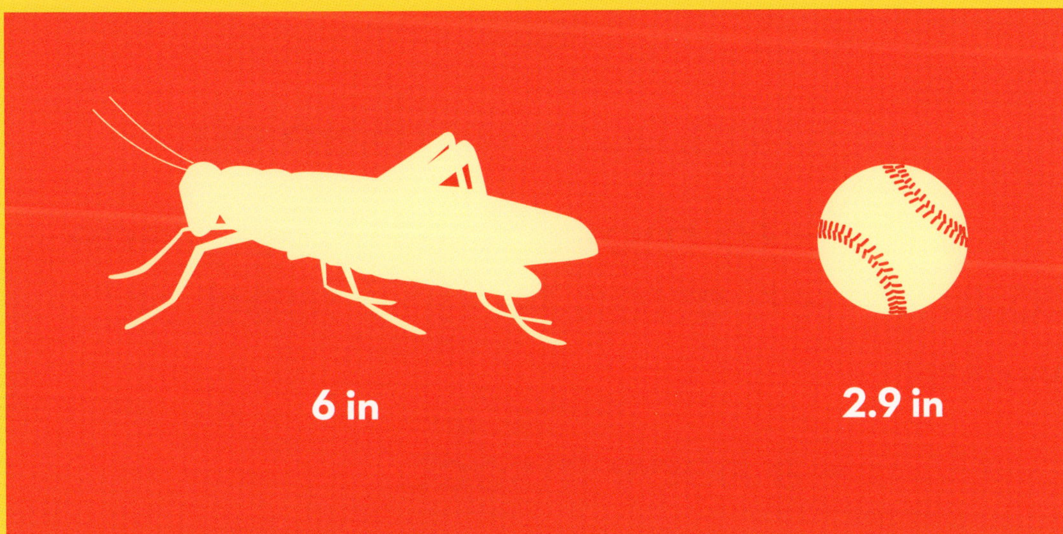

# Glossary

**antennae** - the two long, thin body parts on an insect's head.

**desert** - a very dry, sandy area with little plant growth.

**grassland** - a large area of grass, with few or no trees.

**hatch** - to be born from an egg.

**migrate** - to move from one place to another, often to find food or water.

**nymph** - a baby insect.

# Booklinks

For more information on grasshoppers, please visit abdobooklinks.com

Zoom In on Animals!

Learn even more with the Abdo Zoom Animals database. Check out abdozoom.com for more information.

# Index